Confe

{Con

By Jemima McCandless

Author of Romantic Comedy

Window Shopping For Men:
Buy One Get One Free (BOGOF)

Dedicated to my colleagues past & present

Thank you Tablet Gods for blessing this book.

TABLE OF CONTENTS

PROLOGUE 4

INTRODUCTION...6

Irresponsible Pharmacist 11

Methadone 21

The Addict's Prayer 28

Got Anything for This 29

Mystery Shoppers 39

STRESS...48

Thirty Days has September 55

Over the Counter 65

On the Counter 75

No Word of a Lie 77

White Lies 79

Lottery of Life...85

Exemptions 90

ABUSE 98

Flu Jabs..103

Shit the Bed...106

Health & Safety 117

The Humble Kettle 121

EPILOGUE 122

THE END 125

PROLOGUE

On numerous occasions, usually following some hilarious episode, I've jokingly said to colleagues "We could write a book!"

Well here it is, and my only regret is that I didn't start making notes earlier in my career, but I never anticipated accumulating more anecdotes than I can mentally recall.

The general public never cease to amaze me. Just when I think I've seen it all, in walks "Another one for the book."

What can you expect from this book? What I have come to expect doing my job – the unexpected!

Ever waited for a prescription (patiently or otherwise) and wondered why it takes so long to put your medication in a bag? Confessions of a Chemist will enlighten you, and go some way to dispelling the general misconceptions surrounding what community pharmacists do for a living. *Oh to be a fly on the wall.*

If only I could play you some CCTV footage. As well as seeing us bag-up your prescriptions, you'd see community pharmacists singing; dancing; juggling; praying; crying; laughing…

You'd see that we are not dispensing robots but human beings. Singing and dancing *Gangnam style*. Juggling fruit or boxes of tablets – as well as a heavy workload. Praying, not only for pay a rise but praying for real – on a mat, facing Mecca. Crying, if it's a particularly stressful day, into our lukewarm coffee. But more often than not, you would see us laughing.

As you will read, working with the general public we have a lot to laugh about. Not to mention our pharmacy-specific jokes. *Oh alright then, I'll just mention one.* "Which Anusol cream? The one with hydrocortisone or the **bog** standard one?"

This book however is less about pharmacists and more about customers – my patients.

Did you hear about the pharmacist with a short-fuse? He has no patients! *Patience – get it?* Sorry, I'll stop with the silly jokes.

INTRODUCTION

"Are you a real Chemist?" asks a customer at the counter – surprised to find a pharmacy has popped up inside her supermarket.

"No, I'm a cardboard-cut-out" goes through my mind, but she has a prescription in her hand so I hold that thought, and the target-centred part of me welcomes a new customer.

"As opposed to?" I ask. *A hologram? S*miling politely like I've never heard the question before.

The first time someone asked me "Are you a real Chemist?" was in 2009 when a man was jailed in Florida for making a career out of impersonating pharmacists. *Maybe she wants to see my credentials.*

Besides, I'm not a Chemist, I'm a Community Pharmacist. A chemist has a chemistry degree. I have a degree in pharmacy.

Aspirin

Acetylsalicylic Acid

$C_9H_8O_4$

Despite memorising the chemical structure of Aspirin for my interview with Nottingham University, I have never needed to regurgitate any chemistry during my fifteen years in community pharmacy.

The word 'pharmacist' was around in 1834 according to the Oxford English Dictionary but not commonly used until the later 1800s. And yes ok before that time they did refer to themselves as 'chemists' or 'druggists' but that was over a century ago. *I bet you've stopped calling Snickers bars Marathons.*

So I'm not a chemist. I'm not 'The Pharmacy' either. Don't confuse me with bricks and mortar (pre-fab in the case of some supermarket pharmacies.)

I know it's confusing but the pharmacy is the registered premises where you will find pharmacists at work – working to ensure safe and effective use of medication.

Another thing I am not is a dispenser. 'The Dispenser' is the person who, *how do you put it? "Counts pills all day"* A pharmacist double-checks the medication after a dispenser has dispensed it. I can dispense too but the traditional role of dishing out drugs has evolved. Community pharmacies still dish out a lot of drugs, more than ever before actually (6,500 items on average per pharmacy per month) but over the years we've become healthcare professionals – advising patients and practitioners on drug selection / dosages / interactions / side effects...

"Can I speak to the nurse?" *No. I'm not a nurse.* And no, you can't speak to the doctor either. You'll find them both at your GP surgery. You have wandered under a big green sign saying PHARMACY. "Can I help you madam? **I am The Pharmacist**."

The linchpin of an integrated healthcare service – community pharmacy is often the first point-of-contact for the public. Granted we are not high up in the hierarchy of healthcare professionals, but we aim to please and occasionally we are rewarded with a patient's praise.

Praise that puts us up there with the best of them "You've been ever so helpful. More helpful than my GP even. Thank you."

Most customers say thank you and quite a few shake my hand. Sadly it is not company policy to accept gifts from members of the public, but if you come bearing chocolate NUDGE-NUDGE-WINK-WINK we will eat the evidence. We will not however thank you for unwrapped boiled sweets out of your pocket. That's plain weird. Why would we want warm mint imperials that you've been jingling next to your sweaty balls? *Weirdo!*

Assuming I still have a job after writing my confessions, I am a community pharmacist working in a supermarket pharmacy. My previous employers are many and varied including large multiples and much smaller independent's, but I am enjoying supermarket pharmacy more. I feel less vulnerable to attack (with their in-house security) and the people-watching is first class.

How many people can say they've seen a £30,000 just-thatched Rooney-esk hair transplant up close? He stood out like a sore thumb, asking for painkillers over the counter. You'd be surprised what we see in supermarket pharmacy. We see it all.

Shopping in your dressing gown seems to be on the increase, and not just late at night but Saturday afternoons too! *Would it be illegal and/or unethical for me to photograph customers and post to Facebook?*

But the award for 'the craziest get-up' goes to DRUM ROLL the man on New Year's Eve who came in wearing a kilt and a pirate's hat, casually pushing his trolley, playing a harmonica. *Now I've seen it all.*

Irresponsible Pharmacist

The first thing I must remember to do every morning is put my Responsible Pharmacist notice on display. Conversations about my RP notice on the wall boggle the general public "What were you before 2009 then? An Irresponsible Pharmacist?"

That question is not as stupid as it sounds. I've been a qualified pharmacist for about fifteen years and a 'Responsible Pharmacist' since 2009 when The Responsible Pharmacist Regulations came into force. (Let's not go there.)

Pharmacy assistants are very 'responsible' too. Highly-skilled and under-valued, my Medicine Counter Assistants will for example decide if a product is suitable for you. "Do you take any other medication?" they ask, and they won't accept "Well... Not much" for an answer. "Oh go on then, take them, it'll be alright."

Pharmacy assistants tend to be female. In fact I've only ever worked with one male assistant – who also happens to be one of the best Accuracy Checkers in town. In considering aliases (to preserve the anonymity of my assistants past and present) it dawned on me that in the last six years I've worked with no fewer than six Karens.

Does every pharmacy have a Karen, or three? For the purpose of this book, **I shall refer to all my assistants as Karen**, and I shall not differentiate between Medicine Counter Assistants / Dispensing Assistants / Technicians / Accuracy Checkers...

A community pharmacy cannot open without a Responsible Pharmacist signed in as such. I'm signing in one day and Karen says "You'll never guess what happened yesterday" *A rep brought us lots of pens? You solved the mystery of where all the paperclips disappear to? An inspector came and found my milk in the fridge?*

Turns out the Karens (plural) were waiting for a locum pharmacist to arrive "Where is he? He's late" Meanwhile the locum was waiting (in the queue) for the shop to open.

It was half-past nine before the locum heard two women in the queue tutting "The pharmacist hasn't turned up so they can't open."

Too embarrassed to stand out of the line and announce "HERE I AM are you waiting for me?" the locum sloped off round the corner and phoned the shop to say he was just pulling up – they could open the doors.

Until quite recently, I also had the post nominal letters MRPharmS after my name. Not a qualification or licence to practice, but a mark of professionalism used with pride by pharmacists.

With or without the title I'm a glorified pill counter – right? Regulation of the profession transferred in 2010 from the RPSGB (Royal Pharmaceutical Society of Great Britain) to the GPhC (General Pharmaceutical Council) The Royal Pharmaceutical Society retained a professional leadership role, and MRPharmS is reserved for pharmacists who choose to be a paid member of the society. Can't say I've missed the letters after my name. *I'd miss the £192 more.*

Before RP notices, RPSGB certificates were mounted on the dispensary walls with pride. The public could be excused for thinking the bigger the certificate – the more important the pharmacist. As a newly qualified pharmacist I'd a little A4 certificate to carry from shop to shop, and I was intimidated by the poster-size certificates of the big fish – the pharmacy managers with their RPSGB certificates framed in walnut – as I stuck mine on the wall with *Blu-Tack*.

My career began as a 'relief pharmacist' (locum) in central London. Back then there was a shortage of community pharmacists.

Thinking about it, the term 'relief pharmacist' was probably coined by pharmacy staff waiting for a locum to arrive so they could open up "Oh great. We have a pharmacist. What a relief!"

I'll never forget working on relief. It was on relief that I sold Jesus some throat pastilles! No word of a lie. There I was, working on The Strand, and the lead from Jesus Christ Superstar was losing his voice. *Jesus in his civilian clothes.* Not only that but while working in Victoria Station, I served Saskia from Eastenders in 1999 (bludgeoned to death with an ashtray by Martin Kemp) with something for a 'splitting headache.'

Nowadays there are a few too many community pharmacists and falling rates of pay for locums is indicative of this. I imagine it is a popular degree because you're guaranteed work at the end of it, and the course is not as long as medicine, dentistry or veterinary.

Why did I choose pharmacy? Because I was scared of cows! Seriously, I wanted to be a vet but couldn't get past my fear of cows standing on my toes or charging at me. And living in Cheshire, there are lots of dairy farms and lots of cows.

I was lead to believe pharmacy was a good career choice for a woman (59% of pharmacists in the UK are women) and relatively flexible. Flexible in that women who choose to have a family are able to continue working more easily than in other professions.

Maybe if I take a career break to have a family I'll return to community pharmacy with more appreciation and less cynicism, or maybe I'll use emotional blackmail and cry "Don't make me go back to work"

That said, without my sarcastic wit born out of mild discontent, this book wouldn't be the same.

I'll be honest, I chose community over hospital pharmacy because the pay was more attractive. And I couldn't transfer to hospital now; not without first doing a clinical diploma because over time all the clinical stuff has ebbed away. But I am exceptionally good at checking the accuracy of your medicines as I pop them neatly in a bag and—and all my labels are perfectly straight!

Some members of the public have a preconceived idea (or no idea) of what community pharmacists really do. I know this because you've told me "All you have to do is chuck it in a bag"

Did you seriously think it was as straight forward as bagging up the items listed on your prescription? In a similar fashion to home-shopping colleagues pick groceries to order?

I'll have you know that not only do we generate labels and maintain records of what's dispensed, but we have a fully comprehensive checking process:

Prescription signed by the prescriber? CHECK

Dated? CHECK

Within six months date? CHECK

Can we read the handwriting? CHECK

Have they had it before? CHECK

Is the dosage safe? CHECK

Do the medicines interact? CHECK and so on and so forth…

The first time I ever checked a prescription on my very first day, I'd bagged it up – then had a horrible thought. *Did I check that the labels had the correct patient's name on?*

Opened the bag CHECK

Reseal the bag and hand it to my assistant. "Hang on a minute please" *Did I check the expiry dates?*

Reopen bag. Tip contents onto the bench. CHECK

OK now it's good-to-go!

As a pharmacy manager with a laminated colour RP notice, I'd like to think I'm swimming with the big fish now. Some locums stick up a tatty paper RP notice in black and white – or worse still handwritten! *Have they no shame?* I pride myself on being a good pharmacist and I take the responsibility seriously, but there have been occasions when my professionalism has dissolved into side-splitting hysterics.

"It's a bit embarrassing but I need some advice on farts" says a man in his thirties, already blushing. *If he wasn't red as a beetroot I'd say this was a wind up.*

I show him into the private consultation room. I leave the door ajar and we both sit. "I do have some control over them" he jokes, insinuating I've left the door ajar for ventilation. Seriously, I explain that for my own safety I never shut the door. "I promise not to gas you" he says, starting to look less embarrassed.

"So you have a flatulence problem?" I ask, attempting to keep the conversation serious by using medical terminology. "What's troubling you most about it?" I add, hoping he'll say abdominal pain and swelling. *If he talks about smelly or noisy farts I will crack up.*

"I think I fart too much" he says, and we have a brief discussion about flatulence releasing toxins – better out than in, and all that.

"How much gas is normal?" he asks, and I try to keep a straight face.

"The average man could fill a party balloon with his daily flatus" I answer confidently, as if I'm quoting from a medical encyclopaedia. *Little does he know it was a quote from 'The Little Book of Farting' that mum gave me last Christmas as a stocking-filler.* And we go on to discuss factors such as diet and the importance of chewing your food. "That would be some party trick" he chuckles, when I'm done advising on diet.

"There is one more question" he says, and tells me about his new girlfriend that he's met on match dot com. "As a woman, how long would you say I should wait before introducing flatulence into the relationship?" *For some reason, his use of the word flatulence is even funnier than him saying farts.*

I ask him if they smell bad but I'm barely holding it together by this point. He's my age and we're on each other's wave length. We've built up a rapport in the last five minutes and I feel like I'm advising one of my mates on farting etiquette. *I'm not laughing at him. I'm laughing with him.* He's not taking the piss. He genuinely wants my advice – it's just not the type of advice I'm used to giving as a Responsible Pharmacist.

"Do they smell really bad?" I ask, thinking how *a smelly fart is never truly accepted.* "Well I don't think so, but then I like to pull back the covers and smell my own" he confesses. *Who admits to smelling their own farts?*

"So we're talking about you farting next to her in bed?" I clarify, lowering my-professional-self to his level. And he tells me they've slept together three times now. *If he mentions fanny farts I will laugh-out-loud.* Apparently he's been dashing to the bathroom if he needs to 'let off.'

"Do I still need to hold back?" he asks, trying not to laugh. *When did I become the fountain of flatulence knowledge?*

"You never know, she might be waiting for you to fart first" I say, with tears streaming down my face.

"So your advice would be to let rip?" he asks, offering me his pocket-tissues as I stand to leave the room.

"So long as you don't…" I start to say, but I'm laughing so much I can hardly speak. "So long as you don't hold her head under the duvet" *There I've said it.*

Methadone

For the majority of community pharmacists, after signing in as RP, the first thing on the daily list of things-to-do is to measure out the methadone – before the methadone patients get out of bed.

Preparing methadone can be a chore. I relish not having to do it. Sunday is a nice day to work: we get a lie in on a Sunday, there's no methadone to pour, and it's only a six hour shift. *Happy Days.*

I don't mind Monday's: you can use the weekend as an excuse for under-performance on a Monday. I don't much like Tuesday's: by Tuesday you're expected to be on-form. I like Friday's: I'm doubled up with my job-share pharmacist on a Friday. Saturdays are pretty cool: there's a different, more relaxed vibe to Saturdays. However, there's twice as much methadone to prepare on a Saturday – for the patients to take home Sunday's dose.

Inviting one of our methadone patients into the consultation room, I couldn't help but notice there were police waiting for him outside. "Are they waiting for you?" I ask, handing him his dose of methadone. The green sticky liquid that I measure precisely and watch him consume every day of the week bar Sunday.

He nods as he tries to swallow without gagging. They tell me it tastes disgusting. It's one of the few medicines I've never been tempted to taste.

Putting his hands down his pants, he produces a Kinder-surprise-egg that is full of cream powder. "They're looking for this" he admits, before shoving it back where the sun doesn't shine and leaving the shop.

The police obviously knew he'd concealed it before they caught up with him, but I'm guessing they couldn't arrest him if he had nothing on his person. All we could do, apart from laugh, was stand behind the counter and watch the police test the strength of his anal sphincter – by making him do star jumps and then squats on the pavement outside our shop window!

Experts disagree over what constitutes an addict, but in 2012 there were 197,110 adults in treatment for problematic drug use. Heroin and crack addicts account for 81% of those in treatment.

Heroin is not the root cause of the problem (one in three people suffer from an addiction at some time in their lives) *if it wasn't heroin it would be something else.*

Over the last seven years, the number of young adults in treatment has fallen, but the over-40s are on the up and account for almost a third of those of treatment.

The number of heroin addicts starting treatment has reduced from 47,709 (in 2005/06) to 9,249 (in 2011/12) and almost 30,000 addicts successfully completed their treatment programme during 2011/12. *Does the methadone programme work?* Personally, I've only known a handful of methadone patients get off it. I've known many more addicts stay on methadone for over twenty years.

Methadone was introduced in the 80's to curb the HIV from needle-sharing addicts. It is a synthetic opiate / narcotic analgesic that relieves cravings without the rush that heroin brings the user. Initially the methadone is prescribed at a dose to stop withdrawal from heroin and can be gradually reduced when the time is right. Some say heroin is easier to kick than methadone (which is also highly addictive) but treatment programmes in the UK have tended to focus more on maintenance/abstinence than recovery. Patients on a methadone programme tend to use less illicit drugs and are therefore less likely to commit crime to fund their drug habit. *Whether or not that is an acceptable treatment goal is debateable.*

Swiss clinics allow addicts to inject heroin under medical supervision up to twice a day; getting addicts out of 'needle parks' and reducing drug related crime. The UK has community pharmacists supervise the oral consumption of methadone.

Identical twins 'thick as thieves' both used to get their methadone from me. It was impossible to tell them apart and this always concerned me. No doubt the police had similar issues identifying them – if witnesses to a crime reported seeing "one of the brothers" but couldn't say which brother they'd seen. *I could hardly fingerprint the pair of them.*

Nowadays, pharmacies supplying vast quantities of methadone can purchase Biometric Methadone Dispensers – with roughly 500 methadone-related deaths annually, no-one wants to make a wrong supply. Back then, it worried me that one of the notorious twins could collect methadone twice in one day (by pretending to be the other) and I'd be none the wiser.

According to another methadone patient (who told me this story as it unfolded) the police arrested one of the twins for burglary despite his claiming they had the wrong brother. Sadly the arrested twin (an alcoholic and habitual drug user) died an accidental death (from acute alcoholic poisoning) while in police custody. *Did police arrest the guilty twin?*

At the inquest, the constabulary said "it was a tragic loss of life" and I thought *that could have been me facing the coroner's inquest – explaining a case of mistaken identity.* Always quick to disrespect each other, the methadone patient who was telling me this story said in his opinion "It couldn't have happened to a nicer lad."

Clientele varies with demographics but nowhere is void of drug addicts. It saddens and angers me that some pharmacies turn methadone patients away "We don't stock that. Try down the road."

What happened to a problem shared is a problem halved?

Serving without prejudice can be difficult; especially for pharmacy colleagues who work hard for little more than the minimum wage. They see addicts getting their treatment for free; selling their methadone; addicts who continue to use drugs and alcohol; holiday prescriptions for addicts to take methadone to the Caribbean; addicts driving uninsured old bangers while under the influence…

Is it fair that people who have never paid into the system get it all for free, when patients with dementia spend their life savings on nursing care?

The reality is that quite a few exemptions (from prescription charges) seem unfair.

Europeans who can't speak English are entitled to free prescriptions because they're on benefits. Shaz is claiming disability allowance but doesn't need her wheelchair when we see her down the bingo; John ticks Job Seekers Allowance but he'll never work again because he can make more money selling crack cocaine. And then we've Sir Rolph who bought himself a title but ticks Income Support – we see Sir in the video shop where his boyfriend works.

In a shop with up to 50 methadone patients, I've witnessed all manner of chaos including undercover police pouncing to arrest an addict in my shop; rival addicts stabbing each other in the doorway; drunken addicts kicking off because we can't supply while they're intoxicated; a suicide attempt in the outside toilet; addicts needing to use our rear entrance because someone was chasing them; exchanges of sleeping tablets for puked up methadone. Not forgetting all the light-fingered addicts stupid enough to bite the hand that feeds them.

And while I can't deny that customers and colleagues alike may find some methadone patients to be unsavoury characters, what they don't realise is how easily it could have been their son or daughter needing help. And they do need help. But the stigma runs deep.

Even pharmacists who happily provide the 'supervised consumption of methadone service' might occasionally sneer at the methadone patients behind closed doors – stereotyping the lifestyle of a methadone patient and labelling them all as addicts.

The Addicts Prayer illustrates the stereotyping addicts face. *Pray for change.*

The Addict's Prayer

Our Father who art in prison,
Mother forgets his name.
Thy addiction come,
there's robbin to be done,
on CCTV (we'll join you in prison)
Give us this day our daily meth.
And forgive us our debts,
we'll never repay society.
Lead us not into employment,
but deliver us free housing.
For thine is the addiction,
to crack and to heroin.
Whatever,
innit.

Got Anything for This

Never a dull moment. Often that is what we wish for – a dull moment. The minute I put the kettle on, put a boiled sweet in my mouth or perch my bottom on the stool, someone asks something my assistants can't answer.

"My fallopian tubes are blocked since I went scuba diving" says a muscly man in his thirties. This might have thrown me, like it did Karen, if I hadn't been diving and experienced the post-dive deafness. "Blocked eustachian tubes you say?"

Conversations can start off innocently, but turn disgusting and put me off my lunch. *I'll speak to this lady while the kettle boils.*

"How do I get the poo to flush down the toilet?" asks a customer, with white-floaty-stools associated with taking Alli (for weight loss) and not reducing the amount of fat you consume.

"If the fat is not absorbed it has to come out" I explain "You'll find if you eat less fat it will become less of an issue but I've no idea what you should do in the meantime. You could phone the Alli helpdesk and ask them how to dispose with the poo?" *You can have my salad box if you like. I'm not hungry any more.*

Unless I leave the dispensary, my lunch will be interrupted. "Oh my god what happened to you?" Karen shrieks, as a man with a red swollen head walks into the shop. Earwigging, I heard he'd gone to a fancy dress party as *Shrek* and obviously had an allergic reaction to the green face paint. *Now this I have to see.*

Often I take a break in the consulting room because if I leave the pharmacy premises all trading must cease. The trouble is that patients want to show us stuff in that same room so my lunch still gets interrupted. *There's nothing I'd like more, than to look at your smelly fungus-feet, mid sandwich.* "Yes you're right it is Athletes Foot."

If I do venture upstairs to the staff canteen, colleagues from other departments like to ask me their medical questions "I know you're on your lunch but…" Even on my days off there's no escaping it. I imagine it's the same for doctors if a fellow passenger collapses on-board an aeroplane and you can hardly say "Sorry but I'm on holiday."

If it's not colleagues it's *Facebook* friends or relatives wanting advice on minor ailments. "Do I need to see the doc or have you got anything for this?" asked a friend at a BBQ dropping his shorts in the garden to show me a boil on his bottom.

Confessions of a Chemist

Thankfully, no-one ever shouts "Is there a pharmacist in the place?"

Ever since we got Private Consultation Rooms the public want to show us their embarrassing bodies. Now I don't know about you, but personally if I know the doctor's going to look at my lady-garden I'll be sure to trim the bush. *What is it with patients who don't shave their legs or wash their feet before revealing themselves to me?*

"Can you give me something for a rash?" says a middle aged man who's asked to see me in private. Note: a wise woman once told me to leave the door of the consulting room open – as an escape route – and not to sit down immediately.

"Tell me about your rash." I say, standing just inside the doorway of the consultation room.

"Well, I get a rash on my penis when it's erect" he says, deadpan. *Oh no. Why me?*

"You'll have to show your GP your erection. I deal with pills not penises" I say, leaving the room. *Should I call security?* The man looks genuinely disappointed. Unfortunately perverts don't have 'sex-offender' tattooed to their forehead so we don't take any chances.

Some customers clearly don't know said room exists and choose to reveal themselves over the counter. "No, don't show me! There are sexual-health clinics for that sort of thing."

Too late – he's unzipped his trousers at the counter! *Oh my god. Talk to the hand while I look away.* "Even if I could tell you if they are genital warts, which I definitely cannot do, you should not buy a DIY wart freeze. No."

Evidently some people think we 'count tablets' yet others confuse us with the nurse and would be happy for us to carry out intimate examinations in our consulting room.

One lady wanted me to tell her what this rash was under her arm and when she lifted her top up she was topless! Two tonne of tit nearly took my eye out.

I'm not sure what we did before consultation rooms. *Oh yes I remember* – we measured people for hosiery (support stockings) in stockrooms, and fitted trusses (for hernias) in elevators.

With the advent of smartphones, customers nowadays ask to show me foul photos in the hope I'll make a virtual diagnosis. "What do piles look like? I've never had them before. Can I show you a picture of what it looks like down there?" *Hell. No!*

It is clearly a struggle for the public in deciding where to go and which healthcare professional to ask for advice but it appears the general rule is "If in doubt, find your nearest pharmacy."

With approx. 10,000 pharmacies in England we are very accessible – too accessible sometimes.

Some members of the public interrupt when counselling another customer on the counter. Others shout questions at me through the hatch.

One man had the audacity to walk round the counter and into the dispensary to ask why it's taking so long. *Did he expect to find me sitting on a stool reading Hello magazine while the benchful of prescriptions piled up?*

Managers from other departments come to ask for our help with bizarre scenarios such as small children with leg's wedged in shopping trolleys. And shoppers come to us for help with non-medical problems such as the old man who forgot to put his hand-break on. (He pushed his trolley to his car only to find it wasn't there anymore. It had rolled across the car park into another parked car.)

To be fair, by the time he'd explained this to me he did have a medical problem – he'd pissed his pants!

"Well it could be worse" I said "At least the car park attendant didn't give you a ticket for not parking between the lines." *He never entertains my sob stories – must be the antipsychotic medication he's on.*

In the same way children ask mum when dad says no, patients come to us when the doctor turns them away empty handed.

"Have you seen the doctor about that?"

"Yes"

"What did he advise?"

"Nothing"

And you think I can help because..?

Often I recommend a product and they'll say "I've got some of that at home." *Code for I don't trust your advice or that's too expensive.* Or they'll say "I bought this yesterday and then found some at home" *More likely you found it cheaper at* Home&Bargain.

Of course there will always be people who demand basic painkillers on prescription because they don't have to pay, and you will have heard of the 'worried well' calling 999 for advice on minor ailments… Well the reverse is also true.

The campaign to "**Ask your pharmacist you'll be taking good advice**" needs small print regarding when NOT to present yourself at my counter.

IF your daughter has gone numb down one side of her body – you should have dialled 999

IF since your GP said you were 'slightly jaundice' two days ago, you and your eye balls have suddenly become soooo yellow that a daffodil-personified stands before me – you need to go to hospital.

IF you are leaning on my counter, pale and sweaty, breathlessly asking if this crushing pain could be indigestion – you should have called an ambulance ASAP instead of staggering in here, but I'll call one for you.

IF your arm is so badly broken that the sight of it, bulging out of your skin, makes me throw up – you need to go to A&E and I probably didn't need to see it, but thanks for the memory.

Customers don't always wait around for my advice. They can't wait five minutes until I'm free to talk but they'll take time off work to see their nurse or doctor about their minor ailment *I bet the GP can't wait to hear about your runny nose.* Customers don't always heed my advice either. *Why ask for it in the first place?*

"Do you think I've got frostbite love?" he asks, removing a glove one winter's day and revealing a finger that is blue/black. *Jeez*

"You need to see a doctor. Today. Do NOT leave it until after the weekend" *Don't you watch the Discovery channel? I've seen this on expeditions to the Antarctic.*

"Well, I'll see how it goes. The roads are icy and dangerous" *But you've driven to the supermarket?*

"But your finger could die!"

"I'll do my food shopping and see how it is then" *Unbelievable. Maybe he'll do a Sir Fiennes and saw his own finger off.*

"Your finger probably is dead!"

"Thanks for the advice" *Can you sign here to say if you need your finger amputating it's not my fault.*

If they genuinely want help, I'll help anyone in any way I can. Most of the time however people don't want diet or lifestyle advice; don't want to admit their smokers cough is worsening lung disease; don't want to change their codeine based painkillers for a less addictive alternative…

People openly admitting their problems and asking for help is refreshing. Even if I can't help, I'll know a man that can.

A man in his forties, accompanied by his parents, came to me one day asking for my advice. Sweating, he openly admitted to be withdrawing from drugs and alcohol with three days to wait until his appointment for detox. He couldn't reduce in a controlled manner because he didn't trust himself to have just a little drink and he was seriously concerned his liver disease could kill him (the doctors had warned that one more heavy session could do it.) He honestly didn't know who to turn to and his parents were beside themselves with worry. He looked extremely unwell and I was aware that sometimes alcohol withdrawal can be fatal.

Signposting him to the nearest open clinic, and encouraging not to go cold turkey was the right decision. The next week he returned, again with his parents, to thank me with a bunch of flowers. The doctors I'd referred him to, medicated him there and then. He hadn't had a drink since. And he'd made a special journey to shake my hand. *Signposting the public to another healthcare professional, when they don't know where to turn, is in itself helpful.*

My favourite signposting scenario was a customer who really needed to speak to her vet but decided to phone me first.

"Will my husband be ok? I got up in the middle of the night to get him a painkiller, but in the morning he said he still had a headache and it was then I realised I'd fed him the dog's tablets!"

Mystery Shoppers

Mystery Shoppers secretly evaluate our customer service and report on things like friendliness or how long they waited to be served.

If we leave our name badge at home or in the car, any name badge will do – so long as we don't get marked down by the mystery shoppers for not wearing one. Needless to say you're never without a name badge if your name is Karen.

Providing they can read my name badge, customers use my first name. *I wish I could remember theirs.* If I don't have their prescription in front of me, I'm useless at remembering my customers' names. Eloise talks to me like she knows me while I'm too embarrassed to say I've forgotten her name. *For all I know, her name could be Elsie or Elise or Eliza.*

Some days I'm tempted to wear someone else's badge for a laugh, and see if customers really do know my name.

"We haven't had a locum called Tit have we?" I ask, finding a spare name badge. "It says Jit with a J" says Karen, laughing at me "You tit."

Mystery shoppers report good and bad behaviour. Name badges assist management in dishing out praise and/or dealing with customer complaints. In pharmacy we have a 'no blame culture' to encourage reporting of errors. In my pharmacy we have a 'no blame culture' because we don't know who done it!? Karen served him. It was Karen. Ask Karen. Karen did it. Blame Karen.

The phone rings. *Could be a mystery shopper.* The patient can't get out and collect their prescriptions because of the snow. He's forgetting the roads are impassable both ways. "Even the home shopping vans are grounded" I tell him, and he decides it'll do next week because he's not run out yet. "Is there anything else?" I ask, thinking *perhaps he'd like me to organise an aid-drop.*

Helpful is my middle name – unless you exhibit one of my pet hates. Inc. customers putting coins on the counter when my hand is outstretched; waving prescriptions under my nose when I'm deep in conversation with another customer; demonstrating their cough over the counter without putting their hand to their mouth; continuing mobile phone conversations at the counter; licking their fingers before they pull a note out of their wallet…

"Funny I didn't recognise you with your clothes on" said a man from my gym, without realising how it sounded to the other customers – who probably now think I moonlight as a stripper. "How are you?" I ask. *I expect there's something wrong with them or their loved one – or they wouldn't have a prescription.* When customers ask me "How are you?" it's very tempting to ask what they do for a living. "Good thanks. You're not a plumber are you? I've a problem with my dual-flush."

Serving my old school teachers is a bit strange. *Role reversal.* The one we called 'Darth Vader' who smoked sixty a day. The one who had a nervous breakdown and started throwing chairs round the classroom. The one I had a crush on and still looks good for his age. The one who I know for a fact was sleeping with boys in my class. The one who got locked in a stationary cupboard on the day we all left school… *Seeing what medication they're on can be interesting.*

Serving my old classmates is equally weird. The 'phantom shitter' who got arrested for curling-one-up in the lecture hall. The beauty queen who became addicted to heroin. The teenage mum who never finished her schooling. The one I punched for snogging my boyfriend… *It's interesting to see how they turned out.*

Confessions of a Chemist

One shop I worked in had a terrible transvestite of a customer. Some days he was Nic and some days he was Nicola, and I found it embarrassing that on the days he came in dressed as a woman he just looked like a man in drag.

He'd clearly not gone the whole hog and had his bits or tits done. I presumed he was an indecisive about transgender surgery. That or his wife forbids it. But I wished he'd make his mind up one way or the other instead of claiming he had a sister because we all knew Nic and Nicola were one and the same. I'd love to go back all these years on, and see if he's a better trannie.

Quite often we say "Customers arrive by the bus load" but one day they literally did. "We've been invaded by Germans" said Karen. Actually they were Russian. The orchestra from the Moscow State ballet was touring the country. Word must have spread on their coach that we were selling blood pressure machines for £10 because that's all we sold for about an hour. OMRON machines, and *Strepsils* lozenges bizarrely.

Foreigners usually manage a few choice words of broken English. I don't know about you but if I was in Portugal, with or without a phrase book, I wouldn't know where to start describing vaginal thrush.

One Portuguese customer gave it his best shot by pointing at his wife's nether regions "ITCH e Crème Pussy" and I gave him the thumbs up.

Two famous politicians were due to visit our supermarket, as they do, and colleagues had been cherry-picked by management to welcome Milliband&Balls at the main entrance. We could see the main doors from our counter, and you would have thought the Queen was coming – for all the faffing with the Oatcake displays in the foyer.

Visitors (daren't enter into the unknown) generally give the pharmacy a wide berth and the Karens don't like to miss out on the action. It was mid-afternoon and we were relatively quiet, so I told the Karens they could go and watch the shenanigans unfold.

I had no desire to shake hands with the Labour leader but I'd decided what I'd say if either Ed entered the pharmacy. I would offer them a blood pressure check, and then ask if they knew the cost of an NHS prescription (after Balls said Osborne and Cameron were *two arrogant posh boys who don't know the price of milk*.)

The two Karens did rather stand out (in their brightly coloured PHARMACY fleeces) and so it was no surprise when the Ed's made a bee-line for the pair of them.

The Boss was so flustered, when Milliband outstretched his hand (to the two colleagues he'd not briefed) he introduced the two Karens as "Two of our pharmacy colleagues" and Balls said "Yes. I can see that" *Priceless.*

Fancy having an emotional breakdown on the counter? Come on in!

The lovely lady in her sixties who burst into tears because her husband ran off with a thirty-six year old – she needed a hug.

The girl whose boyfriend had given her Chlamydia for Christmas – she needed a 'contacts card' to present the other girlfriend with.

"Karen will put the kettle on"

A lovely old lady with Alzheimer's, used to frequently forget why she'd come to one pharmacy I worked in. She liked tea with two sugars. Although try asking her if she'd like tea or coffee and she'd just say "Yes" to both. She came in with her husband once. We didn't know she had a husband. She doesn't either. "He's not my husband" she said. "Who is he?" I asked. "He's like my husband but different" she said sweetly. "Your husband won't do the washing up though will he" jokes the ever-loving husband "I have to do it."

Smiley babies, cute kids, attractive people and lovable old folk will all draw me out of the dispensary and onto the counter – no matter what I'm doing. It's amazing what small children can do with our plastic chairs in the customer waiting area. Predictably they stand on them; stack them; walk along them; fall off them; puke on them; throw them; jump off them… But if they do something creative, I might delay telling them their prescription is ready just so I can see what happens next.

One of our regulars has a four year old boy who, if the waiting room is empty, will carefully rearrange the chairs into a perfect arc. *Who said the chairs must be lined up straight against the wall?*

Other customers I'll actively hide from when warned "Hide!" Like the crocodile in Peter Pan we can hear him coming in his mobility car. I have to speak to Dettol-man through the window of his car. He won't get out. There are GERMS. I wouldn't mind speaking to him in person if he didn't phone me every week and ask me the same questions. "Are there any stomach bugs going around? I'm on antibiotics for a chest infection. Will they protect me from anything else?" Not only is he like a broken record, but I know he phones all the other pharmacies and asks them the same thing.

We get funny phone calls. "Angel Delight has turned my wee pink. Should I be worried?"

We get prank callers. "I have strawberries stuck up my bottom. Do you have any cream?"

Ridiculous phone calls are the norm. "Do you hire carpet cleaners?" *Wasting my time.* The Karens are well practiced at filtering calls and time-wasters but "The pharmacist is busy. Can I help?" doesn't always wash.

I'll tell you now (so you can stop calling me) if you spent the evening waiting to be seen in A&E with chest pains but got bored and came home, I can't tell you over the phone if you were having a heart attack or not. *You need your head seeing to.*

Constipated for as long as she can recall (describing her poo to me for the last 18 months) probiotic drinks have made this anonymous caller's stools too soft. *Some people are never satisfied.* We've done the whole stool-sample-in-the-post thing to rule out bowel cancer. I say 'we' because she phoned to ask me what to poo in. Newspaper or a carrier bag or a Tupperware container..? *Retch.* "You could always stop drinking the Yakult?" I suggest.

BE WARNED if you become a persistent caller, asking the same unnecessary questions every week, I will put you on speakerphone!

Not so we can all have a laugh at your expense, that would be unprofessional you understand, it's just so I can carry on checking prescriptions.

The funniest phone call I've ever had was from a woman who was laughing so much I initially thought it was a prank call. Listening more intently, I could hear her husband shouting "It's not bloody funny Margaret."

It clearly was.

"My husband wants me to ask you what he should do (LAUGHTER) he didn't wash his hands after rubbing *DeepHeat* on my back. I thought he'd been a long time in the toilet. I found him in the bathroom (LAUGHTER) dangling his balls in a sink of cold water."

STRESS

What's worse – forgetting to drop off your prescription before you do your grocery shopping, and having to wait on your way out for us to dispense it – or dropping it off when your trolley is empty, and not remembering to collect it until you're unpacking shopping at home?

In a supermarket with a pharmacy near the exit, you might wonder how one could leave the building without remembering their prescription. You would be surprised how many people do. *If only I had a pound for every time it happened.* It doesn't surprise me anymore. I think I know why it happens because it affects us all

INFORMATION OVERLOAD

Antidepressants had the largest increase of any drug group 2010/11 in England – in terms of both the number of items dispensed (3.9 million) and the net cost (£49.8 million) to the NHS.

Community pharmacy is not immune to the 21st century epidemic that is stress. Friends of mine have sobbed before starting their shift, dreading of the day ahead of them. I have gone home and cried on more than one occasion due to the pressure of the job, and I have arrived at work to find the locum in tears after a particularly stressful morning.

It's not my employer. It's not my profession. It's rife. From the Prime Minister who you'd expect to be stressed, to the cleaner you wouldn't, all too often it's part of the day job.

Stress can do funny things.

A delivery of controlled drugs went missing one day. The pharmacist in charge on the early shift had still not found this box of tablets when I arrived for the evening shift. She knew it was missing because we count the controlled drugs cabinet inside-out post Harold Shipman.

She could remember signing for the delivery but she had no idea where she'd put it after that – until she went to watch CCTV footage of her accepting the delivery and bingo.

Thinking she must be losing her mind, she watched herself putting the controlled drug in the fridge!

Pharmacy assistants get stressed too.

One busy afternoon, a customer asked Karen for a free blood pressure check and was duly shown into the consultation room told to take off her coat off and relax.

The pharmacy got busier and you can probably guess what I'm going to say. Everyone had gone and forgotten about the customer waiting for her blood pressure to be checked. Karen had gone upstairs for a fifteen minute break. The customer sat patiently in the room for about half an hour!

No wonder her blood pressure was a little on the high side.

If I had a pound for every pharmacist I've heard say "I love my job" gosh I'd have—about a pound. I don't love it. I don't hate it either.

I do it willingly and well but I am not alone in my pessimism. At least one in three of us are disillusioned with pharmacy and considering leaving the profession. Two out of three would not recommend it as a career. So why has my job become less satisfying, demoralising even?

My answers are probably no different to the next mans.

Too many changes
Too little support
Too much red tape and paperwork
Too little time and energy for customers
Too many targets
Too few support staff
Too heavy a workload

Why have I not left the profession instead of grumbling? Well, frankly it hasn't always been this way. Besides, I enjoy making a real difference to people's lives on a daily basis and I remain genuinely happy to help 99% of the general public 99% of the time.

Still, I'm not likely to encourage you to wait while I dispense your prescription. "Would you like to wait or are you calling back?" asks a newbie Karen. "Don't give them the option of waiting" I coach her. "Ask if they're shopping and give them an idea of how long it might be before its ready."

If a small prescription takes five minutes to dispense, I might add five minutes to the time taken to dispense (in order to ease the pressure) "Ready in ten" whereas a Karen might deduct five minutes (not wanting to displease the customer) "Right away!"

Mr Hurry says "I'm just buying a few bits. I'll only be 5 minutes" *Your prescription won't be ready in five.* "See you in an hour when I've filled my trolley" says Mr Chilled, and we say "Thank you very much." Mr Nice says "I'll be back tomorrow" *Result.* "You can come again"

The Fire Alarm sounds. It is not a drill and the whole supermarket has to be evacuated. I get the keys ready to pull the shutters and lock up as the Karens usher customers out to safety.

For me, assuming no-one is actually on fire, this is a chance to get out in the open air and an opportunity to see firemen in uniform.

For some customers, the fire alarm causes PANIC "When will my prescription be ready?" they ask frantically. *It's not going to do itself, while we're out here on the car park.* "Why don't you collect it after work?" I suggest calmly.

Encouraging you to shop while we dispense your prescription is not a ploy to make you spend money; I just prefer my job when there's no pressure. That's often when mistakes happen – when we're under pressure. Untrained staff can be another catalyst for error. We had a work experience lad once who was super-confident despite never setting foot in a dispensary before. He clearly thought we really did just throw boxes of tablets into a bag!

He correctly transferred a prescription from the counter to a basket, which the dispenser then fills with the relevant tablets ready for labelling, and me-laddo takes it upon himself to pop the boxes into a bag. I swear if I hadn't been watching, he would have just handed it all (including the prescription) back to the customer. Just like that. No labels. No accuracy check. No professional check for drug interactions. No record of the supply. No prescription to know where the patient lives and chase after them…

"This is your first day. Golly gosh. I don't even trust you to make my coffee." I threw the company SOPs folder at him.

Standard Operating Procedures or SOPs define processes within the pharmacy including stuff we shouldn't be doing. For example we've all signed to say we will 'delete the history of *Facebook*' I mean will <u>not</u> use the internet for things unrelated to work. *We all have smart-phones for social-networking anyway.*

We still have some professional freedom, like whether we choose to stick the label on the box or the tube, but we all sign to say we will follow the SOPs to the letter.

Breach of SOPs would be reason for dismal, but try as we might some SOPs are near impossible to follow such as **Use a different colour pen** to sign the 'dispensed by' and 'checked by' boxes on each label. *I'm lucky if I can find* A pen. *They walk.*

These days I have a checklist for all the checklists; most of which are terribly important, but when the cleaning manager came to me with her weekly checklist already filled in – giving the cleaners 100% without having walked the department – that particular checklist became nothing more than a tick-box exercise. *Bureaucratic nonsense.*

I've learnt not to be too nice to cleaners.

One of the cleaners Darren had terrible BO but we regularly wanted him to unclog and empty our industrial size shredder, and so I was always nice to him despite his body odour. Plus Darren had a new mop, and once his BO has followed him out the floor smelt clean like it should. The late-shift of cleaners used an old mop that left the dispensary smelling like wet dog, so I always welcomed Darren into the pharmacy. That was until he asked me on a date! *Seriously? You think there's a chance I'll come down the social club with you?*

Thirty Days has September

Mr Unhappy says "These are the wrong tablets. These are not Lipitor"

And I say "No but Lipitor is atorvastatin Sir. If you look with me here it says atorvastatin underneath Lipitor" as I show him the box that he wants – but can't have since his doctor stopped prescribing the brand.

"Do you see? They're not wrong. It is the same ingredient. Two thirds of all prescriptions are written generically nowadays."

To save the NHS billions of pounds each year, GPs are told to ditch more expensive branded drugs and switch patients onto equally-effective cheaper generic alternatives. In 2011 alone £200 million was unnecessarily spent on two types of costly statin drugs when cheaper alternatives were available.

"I want Lipitor. It's what I've always had"

"Yes but now a generic is available we have to give Atorvastatin unless the doctor writes Lipitor on the prescription" *or we lose over £20 a box*. "Generic tablets are as effective as the well-known brand" I add.

He asks if I buy *SmartPrice* cornflakes or *Kelloggs*. "You can't compare medicines to cornflakes" I argue.

"Basically you're giving me the cheap stuff now" *Admittedly atorvastatin is under £2 for a month's supply.*

"That doesn't mean it's not as effective as the Lipitor" *at £25 a box.* I try to reason with him "You could ask your doctor…" but Mr Unhappy huffs "Next time I'll take my prescription elsewhere."

Why don't doctors warn their patients?

Some patients struggle to comprehend why tablets come in packets of 28. "Why do they make a pack size of 28 when February is the only month with 28 days in it?" *Why do you think?* I know that 30 days has September, April, June and November. All the rest have 31 except February alone which has 28 days…

Do you seriously expect manufacturers to produce a variety of different pack sizes of 28, 30, 31 and 29 every four years? And for me to then ask you what months (and corresponding pack size) you need the supply for? Why is it so hard to grasp the concept of a four-week-cycle? I don't get why you don't get this.

Comically, some doctors must give in to patient-pressure because we do see random quantities of 30 prescribed. *Come on, we've all learnt our 28 times-table now.*

If you run out of your tablets, we can issue up to 30 days' supply in an emergency – assuming we know which tablets you're on about. 'White tablets about so big' doesn't give us much to go off. If we don't trust you or your doctor to furnish a prescription we might just give you five day's supply. And if we don't like you or your attitude, we might charge you for the emergency supply. "Yes I realise you don't pay for prescriptions but you don't have a prescription."

"Can you lend me some diabetic test-strips?"

"Is it an emergency?"

"Yes. I forgot to order my prescription"

"Are you insulin dependent?"

"No but I am diabetic"

"Diet controlled?"

"Yes"

"I can test your blood sugars if you're concerned"

"That's not what I'm asking for"

"Well I'm not sure it's an emergency, and you can buy a box of ten strips for £6.49" I say, knowing full well the minute he discovers it'll cost him he'll decide it's no longer an emergency. *Abracadabra!*

"No thanks. I can wait two days for my prescription" *Watch what you eat and you'll be fine.*

We never assume the prescription which a patient hands in is actually theirs, and I don't mean they're the patient's representative. Dentists' receptionists can write the wrong name and/or address (dentists are too busy to write out all of the prescription) Hospital receptionists can stick the wrong patient's sticker on the prescription. Doctors' receptionists can hand out the wrong prescriptions.

Patients never notice this. In fact, if you couldn't prove it (by showing them their signature on the back) they'd swear blind that wasn't the prescription they handed in! And look at me suspiciously – like I'm a magician with a pack of cards, mysteriously revealing their signature on the Ace of Spades.

Needing to speak to a mum about her son's prescription, I called out "Samuel David James Anthony?" and she said "Yes this is Sam."

Patients' names are a source of constant amusement for me.

What parent would call their son Richard Head? Famous names like Shania Twain. Funny names like Mr Horsfallen. Unpronounceable names, that I give Karen to hand out, like Zwetschnikow. Ridiculous names like Alan Allen. Cheesey names like Sunshine Bright. My favourite is Mr Lightfoot who looks to be about 20 stone.

Patients often walk up to the counter and say nothing but their surname. "**Allcock**" says an arrogant man to Karen, who diligently finds his prescription from earlier. All of us keep stum until he's out of earshot when three of us hoot in unison

"And no balls?"

Even if it was not me that served them initially I'm expected to know what they've returned for. "Swallow" she says. *You can't swallow? You've swallowed something?* "Oh your name is Swallow. Have you dropped off a prescription?" I ask.

Some patients let on they've returned for a prescription but still don't give us enough to go on. "Prescription for Smith" he says, and I'm thinking *any old Smith? I've got lots here. Are you bothered which one you get?*

We don't call out a patient's address because they'll say 'yes' to anything if you're looking directly at them.

The nicest address I've come across is 'Rainbows End' (a cottage) but the best address I've seen is 'The Holy Inadequate' (a pub) *See you at church on Sunday.*

Addresses for daily patients become ingrained to memory but we still have to ask the question "What's your address please?"

"Let's-be avenue" was the usual reply from Martin, a methadone patient bored with the monotony of collecting day-in-day-out. "Would you like to come for tea now you know where I live?" and "If I give you my phone number as well, will you call me?" are both favourites with the single men. One man even brought me flowers when I was working late one Valentine's Day. Nice of him to do so but I shredded his number.

Prescriptions can be interesting too – believe it or not. Curiously, we have at least two Mr & Mrs on the exact same medication – like they've come out in sympathy for each other. *Ah*

I'm always on the look-out for forged or fraudulent prescriptions with amended quantities or items added by the patient... And it's very exciting when I spot one because I can claim a £70 reward from the NHS Counter Fraud Dept.

And we dispense private veterinary prescriptions with inhalers for dogs, contraceptives for chimpanzees, Viagra for cats... All very interesting – not that the cat had erectile dysfunction, but while we're on the subject of ED medication:

One man admitted to selling the little blue pills at work – he's not had sex since 1985.

Another made us note on his records that **under no circumstances must his wife find out he gets Viagra**.

Then our Number One Attractive Customer (who could easily be some Italian footballer on a *Head&Shoulders* advert) disappointingly presented his prescription for Viagra and ticked income support.

Running low on our stock of Viagra, I handed a next man a slip to call back for another box and he innocently said "Can you make a note of my phone number in case I forget to come."

Then, when we'd run out, a Karen in-training offered to borrow Viagra from a nearby pharmacy if he was desperate!?

Patients Medication Records can include pop-up notes to supply the UK product. (As well as do not tell his wife he's on Viagra)

If they're not bilingual, I understand patients not wanting a calendar pack in a foreign language.

(The same drug sells for a different price in the EU and is sometimes cheaper to import = parallel imports.)

We get irrational demands too. Take for example the lady who expects us to keep 6 months stock of her HRT.

"You never have it all in stock. I always have to come back" she says. *What? Twice a year?*

We keep enough to last her three months but that's not good enough. *Some people just love complaining.* "Would you like us to collect your prescription from the doctors in future so we can have it all ready for when you come in?" I suggest.

"No. I like to do it myself. I'm not elderly or infirm" she says.

"No. I just thought you might be busy. We go to your surgery every day. We're open evenings and weekends…"

Community pharmacists are organised professionals. We order repeat prescriptions seven days in advance – anticipating problems and allowing time to put things right before you show up.

Scripts go missing, or end up at the wrong pharmacy. Scripts come unsigned or not legally complete. Items might be missing or the wrong items issued… We genuinely want everything to be spot-on for when you come to collect.

Would you spend half an hour grocery shopping, discover there's only one tin of baked beans left on the shelf, and give up? Take your trolley to customer services and expect them to put it all back on the shelves because you're going elsewhere?

That's what some patients do when we we're one box short of their shipping order. They'd have enough to last them a month, but no. I've come to the conclusion some people like being pedantic. *I hope you go elsewhere and find they've got plenty of beans but no bread.*

"That's not a prescription. That's a repeat slip. Tick what items you need, take it to your surgery and they'll issue a prescription." I explain.

"So I can't get it from here?"

"If you give us three days we can drop it at the surgery for you, and pick it up two days later when it's ready" I offer.

"So I can't get it now?" *Is it me or..?*

Patients are supposed to tick what items they require on their repeat slip and the surgery issue a prescription accordingly.

A lovely patient of mine writes an essay every month under the one item on his repeat slip.

We fondly refer to him as Steptoe because his car has corrugated iron where the rear window used to be. Steptoe borrows a clipboard and sits writing a letter to his doctor in beautifully neat handwriting. I'd love to know if his GP retained all the slips.

One man's life story on repeat slips:

Dear doctor, you'll be pleased to know I'm feeling much better. The longer days and light nights help. I keep taking the tablets. Since last month I've started gardening again. I went to M&S and treated myself to some new trousers. Oh and I managed to finish that big jigsaw I told you about last month...

Over the Counter

There will always be those customers who have no shame.

Like the girls from the 'massage parlour' down the road who are buying lotions for scabies along with their baby oil.

But usually embarrassing purchases are "for someone else" unless of course they're looking for XL condoms. "Extra strong too"

From my counter, I've seen what happens to men who purposely go through self-scan checkouts to avoid the embarrassment of buying condoms from an assistant – entertainingly, the alarms go off at the main entrance because the condoms haven't been de-tagged by a checkout operator! *How red will this one go, waiting for a security guard to walk their embarrassing purchase to the deactivator and back?*

Every other customer requests the codeine based painkiller co-codamol. If it's not co-codamol it's a tablet to aid sleep. Lifestyle advice might cure their insomnia but only if they admit they have a problem. "They're not for me."

Some requests are for both. *Yes we know, the co-codamol is for you and the sleep aid is for someone else.*

Patients should not use co-codamol for more than three days or they risk becoming addicted to the codeine and dependency on opioid analgesics is a real concern. "Yes. I've taken them before. Yes. I only take them occasionally" *The fact you anticipate my questions parrot fashion indicates to me you purchase regularly.* Medicine counter assistants have a duty to warn every customer about the three day guidance. "THREE DAYS? I've been taking them for thirty years love!" But not every customer appreciates their concern.

"I work in a GP surgery" *You could be the tea lady for all I know.* Or "I'm a nurse" is another common snub. *You should be pleased we're giving the correct advice shouldn't you?*

If anyone ever admitted to being dependant on them we could recommend a less addictive painkiller but that's only happened to me once in fifteen years.

Medicine Counter Assistants are trained to sell no more than one packet per customer of certain medicines. Paracetamol is one such ingredient and pseudoephedrine (decongestant) is another.

Paracetamol sales were restricted to reduce the incidence of overdose. Decongestants (colds/flu/sinus) were nearly taken off sale altogether when police discovered people were cooking crystal meth (illicit drug) from pseudoephedrine in their kitchens.

Assistants rightly refer requests for multiple sales of paracetamol-containing products to me. Firstly, I didn't make the rules. Secondly, my assistants wouldn't be doing their job if they didn't refer to me. Thirdly, it's not all about you. The bigger picture includes 70,000 intentional self-harm incidents involving paracetamol overdose and is the most common cause of acute liver failure. "But I'm not going to kill myself" they argue. *Would you admit it if you were?* I can imagine how that conversation would go:

"Can I buy two packets of paracetamol?"

"Are you planning on taking an overdose?"

"No but I appreciate you asking"

"Well, in that case yes. Have three packets!"

If we don't think it's safe, we can and will refuse sales even if you back-peddle!

Telling Karen your child is five, but when the cough mixture is only suitable from six years, you try telling me your other child is seven. *And you expect me to believe that?*

Even if YOU know what you need, we might refuse the sale.

We frequently get customers requesting medicines for animals, when we cannot sell 'medicines intended for human use' for animal use.

We sell worm and flea treatments for cats and dogs. We sell sample bottles to a lady who rescues hedgehogs (and samples their stools for worms) but it is illegal to sell human medicines for animal use – even if your vet told you to buy it!

We know veterinary medicines can cost an arm and a leg, but once you tell us it is for animal use we have to refuse the sale.

"Is it a dry or chesty cough?"

"Difficult to tell really. It's for my horse"

"Oh I can't sell you a cough mixture for your horse"

"The Vet told me to buy it"

"Well I'd be breaking the law"

"This is ridiculous. Just sell it to me!"

"NO. Not only is it illegal but there are no directions on the bottle for horses. You could sue me if something went wrong"

"Oh now you're being petty"

"I'm not risking my job for your horse"

"Fine. I'll go elsewhere and say it's for me."

I shout after him "How will you know how much to give Dobbin?" but he's already left the building.

I've developed super-human hearing (from years of listening to what Karen's selling over the counter) and I've perfected the art of shaking a box of tablets (instinctively knowing whether is it a full or a split pack) but I don't have a crystal ball.

"I've tried one tablet and it didn't work."

"Which tablet did you try already?"

"I don't know I can't remember."

What if I sell you the exact same tablet?

"Do you take any other medication?"

"Yes how long have you got? Don't ask me what they're all called"

"Do you have a list of your medication?"

"No"

"Without knowing what you take, I'm afraid I can't safely recommend anything"

"So you can't recommend anything then?"

Count to ten.

"Can you order my moisture cream?"

"Yes. Which cream?"

"Oh what's it called?"

"Have you got the box?"

"No, I've thrown it away"

"I don't know then I'm sorry"

"So you can't order it for me then?"

Not unless you're happy for me to take a guess.

"Did you read the article in the Daily Mail?"

"No, was it good?"

"Yes. I wanted to discuss it with you"

"Have you got it with you?"

"No"

"What did it say?"

"I can't remember exactly"

Maybe that should form part of a pharmacist's terms of service 'I promise to read all medical articles in the Daily Mail'

Usually I'll back up what my assistant says, but occasionally I'll let you have whatever you want.

"Can I have some thrush cream please?" asks an old man at the counter and Karen asks "Is it for a lady?"

"No, it's for my wife"

"We can't sell it for ladies over sixty"

"Well she's not a lady"

"Is she over sixty?"

"YES and she needs cream for her FANNY"
(Raising his voice)

"Well she'll have to go and show it to her doctor"

"Can I see the pharmacist" he insists, and I'm there in a flash because I've been listening
(and trying not to laugh)

"Can I buy some anti-fungal cream for my foot please?" says the old man
(who doesn't realise I've been listening)

"Yes" I say, while thinking *I mustn't make a fool out of Karen because she was quite correct.* "Yes I'll sell it to you but your wife needs to make an appointment to see her GP"

"What for?" he asks, with a puzzled look on his face.

Confessions of a Chemist

"Her fanny"

RING-RING-RING-RING

"Is that the pharmacist? Do you remember me? I've just bought some ibuprofen for my daughter's earache and I'm phoning to ask how long must she lie down for? How long will it take for the syrup to work its way to her ear?"

"It should start to relieve her pain within the hour. Have you given her a spoonful of paracetamol too?"

"What? At the same time? In the same ear?"

"You've lost me"

"On top of the spoonful of ibuprofen in her ear?"

Oh my...

Confessions of a Chemist

On the Counter

Two chavs came in for advice one evening. I'll call them Dumb and Dumber. It was obvious as he approached the counter that Dumb had a red eye. He wanted some eye drops, but on questioning his eye was painful and he had photophobia.

"You need to go to the walk-in centre tonight" I said.

"Why can't you sell me some drops?" asked Dumb.

"Because your eye is painful and you don't like bright lights" I explain.

"His eye is not normally like this" says Dumber. *Obviously.*

"Would you **not** go to A&E with a broken arm because it's **not** normally like this?" I asked Dumber.

Then Dumb pipes up "I've got to go to work tonight" to which I reply "I'm sure they'll understand if you tell them you're at the hospital."

So off they go.

But ten minutes later they're back at my counter the pair of them.

"I'll be late if I go to the hospital" pleads Dumb.

"Can you really not give him owt?" asks Dumber.

"No I really can't. Listen if you go blind you won't have a job to go to tomorrow" I say, trying to shock Dumb into action. At which point Dumb puts his leg on my counter

"Does this make any difference?" he asks, revealing his electronic-ankle-tag.

I was dumbfounded!

Confessions of a Chemist

No Word of a Lie

I've had a distressed mother show me bits of threadworm in a sandwich bag. *Gross!*

I've been asked if paracetamol tablets contain aspirin and I've been asked for disposable aspirin. *To dispose of by drinking after dispersing in water?*

I've been told a lady was putting Cupranol in her ears for wax – she meant Cerumol ear drops. *Isn't that what you paint the fence with Cupranol?*

I've been asked if we sell Fox cream – they meant Tiger balm. *Not cream for foxes.*

I've been asked about Polystyrene sachets for cholesterol, rather than Colestyramine. *I knew what they meant.*

I've had a man referred to me by his 'Triangle nurse' – presumably after he'd been triaged. *About a ringing in his ears?*

I've been asked if capsules can go in a pill box when the original container has a delicatessen in the lid. *A desiccant more likely.*

I've had a man return a TENS machine, after the birth of his baby, complaining that pressing the buttons at every contraction had given him sore thumbs! *I hope you didn't tell that to the mother of your child.*

I've been asked for non-drowsy sleeping tablets, but he immediately realised he'd said something stupid and explained he meant ones that wouldn't make him drowsy the following day.

White Lies

Security systems in supermarkets are top notch – with CCTV cameras that can read the serial number on your £10 note. Having security guards close at hand is very reassuring. I feel much safer than I ever did managing an independent pharmacy on the high street – getting called out in the middle of the night because drunks have smashed the shop window… And from behind our pharmacy counter, we witness all sorts of criminal activity in the supermarket.

From Eastern Europeans stealing £100 worth of chewing gum (to take home and sell on the black market) to health-conscious thieves robbing blood pressure meters, and everything in between. Trolley push-outs usually get caught on the car park, and the thieves have 'the walk of shame' back to the security office. *Ooo look, what did they try to get away with?*

A legless man (not without legs) had been round the supermarket in his mobility scooter, and attempted to drink-drive straight out – passed security – without paying. Had he not been drunk he probably could have driven off but he collided with the alarm barrier!

Security were prepared to let him go after making him pay for the shopping in his basket, but the alarms went off again when he attempted exit number two. Not because he'd driven into the barrier for a second time – he'd stuffed a watch down his coat while he was at it. *Was he planning to drive on the roads in that state?*

The Road Traffic Act doesn't apply to mobility scooters. This loop hole has meant that drink-related incidents involving mobility scooters come under Section 12 of the Licencing Act 1972 which states 'it is an offence to be in charge of any carriage, horse or cattle when drunk' *What century is this we're in?*

I'd like to think we're the honest type, but to be perfectly honest pharmacists don't always speak the truth.

If you're told I'm 'not accredited' to supply you with Viagra under the counter, it's because I don't feel comfortable asking "Do you have trouble achieving and maintaining an adequate erection for penetrative sex?" *Sorry to let you down.*

If you're told we've 'run out of flu-jabs until next week' it's because I can't face doing any more today.

If you want to drug your child to sleep with Phenergan syrup, we've all got very good at looking into empty cupboards with expressionless faces.

Confessions of a Chemist

If you're told we can't obtain Kaolin and Morphine anymore, that's because it's easier not to stock it than deal with people who abuse it (by letting the powder settle and drinking the opiate.)

Customers can be too honest
>> my wrinkly-nose expression

"Can I get something for my wife's vaginal thrush or does she have to come in herself?"

"You can buy it. How do you know it is definitely a yeast infection?"

"It tastes funny"

Too much information.

Tipping exactly 112 tablets onto the counting triangle is like a hole-in-one at golf. *I'm off to buy a lottery ticket*. If I count 111 tablets and that's all we have but your prescription is for 112, I trust you never count them.

If we had 112 but I drop one, well that might depend if anyone seen me drop it.

Of course the 'three second rule' is hearsay. The tablet goes straight in the bin for incineration – assuming they're as cheap-as-chips. If however the tablets are specially-ordered super-expensive tablets then the five second rule may apply.

The 'five second rule' is not hearsay. We hold the dropped tablet for five seconds, blow on it while deliberating, and then bin it – of course.

I'm pretty good at calculating the correct dosage. I spotted an error once where a doctor prescribed a dose fit for 16kg yet the baby was only 16 lbs. (It is my job to check dosages and I'd have been in as much trouble as the doctor if I hadn't spotted it.)

But if you slip in the door two minutes before we close, presenting a hospital prescription requiring dosage calculations with handwriting that looks like a spider crawled across the paper, and I'm so exhausted after my 12 hour day that I can barely remember my own name... I might have to tell you a little white lie. Hmmm *I'm not putting my job and/or your life in jeopardy* so "I'm afraid we'll have to order this in for tomorrow."

Any customers waving prescriptions seem to get past Security after closing time.

They wouldn't let someone with a two-page shopping list start grocery shopping at one minute to never mind one minute past closing time! *That's why we turn the light off at two minutes to.*

With two minutes to go, I also refuse to answer the phone in case you delay my departure. And if you ring before we are officially open, I'll either ignore it (the CCTV cameras can't hear me ignoring a customer) or pretend to be the cleaner.

Speaking of cleaners, one unplugged the fridge (wasting two thousand pounds worth of stock) and we used that excuse for a while "We haven't got your insulin in stock. The fridge packed up sorry. Blame the cleaner…" *If the truth be known, it wasn't the cleaner it was Karen!*

I have your best interest at heart.

A man in his fifties asks if we sell water tablets for swollen ankles. I ask him the usual questions including "Has it happened before? Do you take any prescribed medication?" and I'm not happy with what he's telling me.

I explain with genuine concern that I think he should see his GP and that it's not normal for ankles to suddenly swell, but I can't physically drag him to the doctors.

I tell him we don't sell anything, which is not a complete lie because the herbal diuretics are in the supermarket, and I'd really rather he sees his doctor.

"Thanks but I'll be waiting two weeks for an appointment. I'll put my feet up when I get home" he says.

I have a last ditch attempt to get him there "Tell the receptionist that I said you need to see a doctor." *Like that'll influence the gate-keepers decision not.* "Please go to the doctor. It could be your heart"

"How can it be my heart? It's my ankles!"

Lottery of Life

"A lucky dip lottery for tonight"

"Next counter along" I say "This is the pharmacy" (next to the kiosk selling lottery and cigarettes)

"*20 Benson&Hedges* please"

"Come here when you want to stop smoking"

And when they do come for help in stopping smoking, it tickles me that smokers who were finding £8/day (for one packet of fags) moan if they have to pay a prescription charge of £7.65 for a week's supply of their Nicotine Replacement Therapy or NRT.

I've helped hundreds of patients stop smoking in my time. I wish I could help my mum to stop but they've got to want to stop. I know of smokers who've lost a leg due to smoking-related disease and still don't want to try and stop.

Mr Intense wanted to stop. He came to my smoking cessation clinic for just under a month. *Always immaculately turned out and clearly into his male-grooming*. Interestingly he was smoking forty a day, but coped fine without his fags in smoke-free areas like the cinema or flying long haul.

Diagnosed with personality disorders including Obsessive Compulsive Disorder, the first time he met me Mr Intense said he anticipated becoming addicted to the NRT much in the same way he thought obsessively about his next fag. But he was serious about stopping smoking. He'd memorised all the quirky facts, such as 'the equivalent of a jumbo-jet full of people dying every day, from smoking-related diseases.'

Patches didn't give him anything to do with his hands so Mr Intense continued to smoke. Chewing gum only lasted three days because he had hiccups non-stop. Week three I decided to try him with a nasal spray. *Surely he won't want to use a nasal spray more often than he has to.* Wrong! He'd stopped smoking but he was coming in every third day for more sprays.

I phoned the service manager for advice on dealing with Mr Intense and his overuse of nicotine nasal spray, but before his next appointment he came to see me. And I was about to say "Look I'm sorry but you shouldn't have run out yet" when he said he wouldn't be coming to see me again.

"It's not what you think" he said "I've stopped smoking. I'm addicted to scratchcards now!"

Confessions of a Chemist

Mr Intense had a five-a-day scratchcard habit and was allowing himself to scratch at 10am 1pm 4pm 7pm and 10pm every day. *That's lucky because I didn't know how best to help you.* And off he went to the next counter along for his lottery scratchcards.

It's hard to tell how often our health promotion materials have the desired effect, but I know of one time.

A little boy noticed our smoking cessation display and I heard him shout "Look mummy that's you. Mum, come here. That's you that is" pointing at the picture of a lady surrounded by exhaled smoke. And she followed her son to look. And she went away with some NRT.

Despite us promoting healthy lifestyles, some patients are intent on killing themselves.

Community pharmacists at one time delivered Oxygen cylinders to patients' homes. Home oxygen therapy, it will not surprise you to learn, carries a risk of fire and burns if you smoke in close proximity.

I used to deliver cylinders to a man in his sixties who needed oxygen day and night for lung disease. One time I noticed his mask had one too many holes in it and asked if he'd like me to replace it.

"Get off woman" he snapped, and I listened in disbelief as he explained "I pierced an extra hole in the mask for my cigarette" *Maybe he'd decided that smoking wasn't killing him quickly enough and upped his game.*

Being a good pharmacist does not always = happy customers

More and more customers are asking us for electric cigarettes. Their safety and effectiveness is controversial but the public perceive them to be safer than smoking because e-cigarettes do not contain tobacco. They mimic real cigarettes by delivering nicotine in vapour from nicotine infused water hence the term 'vaping' and while I am all for people stopping smoking, the evidence is lacking.

They are not regulated medicines like nicotine patches and inhalators... More trials are needed. The NHS (including pharmacists) cannot endorse them until they're approved by the MHRA Medicine and Health products Regulation Agency and until that time we can only recommend well-established methods.

Admittedly, The Royal College of Physicians said "the use of NRT including e-cigarettes is many orders of magnitude safer than smoking" but they don't sell them – they can't be sued.

Confessions of a Chemist

And in a world where you'll be sued for giving the wrong advice, is it any wonder healthcare professionals stick to evidence-based treatments? But the people asking for the e-cigarettes are not happy. Some people get really angry because we don't stock them.

When that faced with an angry demand for e-cigarettes, I'm tempted to use scare tactics and tell them about the man in Florida. He was happily 'vaping' when the battery exploded – knocking out his front teeth and part of his tongue; showering red hot metal across the room and setting it alight!

But as one bright spark pointed out "Considering this is only one isolated non-fatal incident among millions of e-cigarette users (and more than one person dies each year in Britain testing batteries on their tongue) customers might very well choose a one-in-a-million risk of injury vs. a 33% chance of dying if they continue to smoke."

"We don't stock e-cigarettes sorry"

Exemptions

(From Prescription Charges)

"The first of April, doesn't time fly? How much have they gone up this year?" asks Mr Gullible, as he signs the back of his prescription.

"Haven't you heard? The Government has abolished prescription charges!" I say.

"Really?" he gasps.

"No sorry. April Fools" I jest.

England is the only country in the UK still charging for prescriptions. You could argue that charging for prescriptions goes against the founding principle of the NHS being free at the point of use.

The Department of Health would argue that (with the extensive exemptions we already have in place) only 10% of prescription items are chargeable anyway. A spokesperson for the DOH said "Abolishing prescription charges in England would leave the NHS with a funding gap of over £450 million a year."

Don't shoot the messenger! Go to Wales if you're that bothered or rally your local Member of Parliament about prescription charges. *Anyone would think the £7.65 lines my pockets!*

Confessions of a Chemist

*M*aybe you would prefer to pay the basic cost of your medicines? "You could ask your GP for a private prescription so you're just paying the cost of you medicine" *without funding the NHS. It's not like it's short of cash or anything.* This patient might feel better about paying £7.65 if I told them their inhalers cost £59 each but that would be unethical.

Some NHS patients accept the charges.

"That will be £15.30 for two items please"

"No Buy One Get One Free offers?" *HaHa*

Some don't want to pay a penny.

It's not my fault that you brought a private hospital prescription into the community. "Yes I know you don't pay for prescriptions but this is not an NHS prescription. If you go back to the hospital you won't have to pay but otherwise I will have to treat it as a private prescription and charge you £2.50 because it's not an NHS prescription."

Is £2.50 really worth splitting hairs over? It'll cost you more than that to pay to park at the hospital.

Some moan about proving they're exempt.

'Point of Dispensing Checks' were introduced 1st April 1999 and have reduced pharmaceutical patient fraud by 60% saving £70 million.

"Print the name of the person who gets the benefit" says Karen, my highly-skilled hard-working assistant. Karen, who is relatively poorly paid (earning less than £8/hr on average) and generally under-appreciated, listens to the public moan about filling in the reverse side of their prescription. *Is it really too much trouble? You should try working!*

"Can you fill in this bit as well for me please?" Karen says, pointing to the box for the name, date of birth, and NI number of the person in receipt of that benefit.

"No-one has ever asked me to do that before" comes the reply, as if we should just take their word for it.

Part of our Terms of Service, pharmacies are required to ask patients for proof – evidence to support their claim of eligibility for help with prescriptions. We ask each and every customer, for evidence of their exemption, each and every time. So don't give me that old chestnut "They don't make me to do that in my local chemist."

Sometimes patients tick the wrong box:

"How long have you got to go?"

"I'm not pregnant. What have I ticked? I have a medical exemption"

I never set out to offend customers:

"Does your dad pay for his prescription?"

"That's not my dad he's my husband"

Sometimes it just happens:

"It's my partner's prescription"

"Does she pay for prescriptions?"

"Yes HE does"

But I give complements too:

"You don't look sixty MrsYoung. What's your secret?" *Oil of Olay?*

"Pile cream dear. Preparation H"

And every customer has a story to tell:

"I'm getting this for my neighbour, a Health&Safety Inspector. He slipped at work yesterday. Broke his leg in two places!" *Ooo the irony. I wonder if he'll put in a claim blaming himself.*

Customers 'pull the wool' all the time:

Mr Benefit Cheat comes in with his prescription after work, still wearing his grease-monkey overalls, and proceeds to tick 'Jobseekers Allowance' *Been doing some voluntary work at your local garage? I could use an honest car mechanic. Do you do foreigners for free too?*

We report NHS fraud:

Dishonest patients may amend quantities, add items the GP refused to prescribe, tamper with or forge prescriptions...

I've supplied boxes of elastic-bands to a dodgy bloke with a forged prescription for strong painkillers. I was waiting for the police and I just couldn't stall him any longer without it looking sus.

Luckily the police pulled up just in time to stop Mr Dodgy legging it with his elastic bands. He literally bounced off the bonnet of the police car.

We cross a box if evidence is not seen:

It is a criminal offence for patients to 'tick the wrong exemption' and/or made a false claim.

Confessions of a Chemist

If found guilty, the NHS will charge them up to £100 (five times the amount they wrongly claimed) plus the charges they should have paid in the first place. 160,000 such penalty charge notices have been issued since 2001.

Can I make it known that the pharmacy profession did not decide the exemption categories – which are completely outdated now. We know there are inequalities.

Please don't shout at me about paying for your antidepressants when medication for an under-active thyroid is free / Hormonal Replacement Therapy carrying not one but two charges when the contraceptive pill is free / asthmatics pay but diabetics don't / two charges for hosiery (one charge for each leg) even if you're an amputee. *I didn't make the rules.*

Was it a man who ruled tights would not be allowed on the NHS only stockings? If so, was it sexually motivated or was he trying to cut the cost of vaginal thrush to the NHS? And why does this rule still stand that men are allowed a suspender belt on the NHS but women are expected to own one?

If the exemption categories are ever up for revision, I shall put forward two new exemption categories: LAZYITIS and ALLERGIC TO WORK.

885 million prescription items were dispensed by community pharmacies in England 2011/12 (up 4% on the previous year) with an average net ingredient cost of about £9 per item, and the average number of prescription items per head of the population was 18.3 items in 2011.

Twenty years ago inhalers and antibiotics were the most commonly prescribed drugs. Nowadays cardiovascular (heart and blood pressure) drugs dominate the top ten.

From the top: Simvastatin (cholesterol) Aspirin (heart attack/stroke prevention) Levothyroxine (under active thyroid) Omeprazole (stomach acid) Ramipril (heart/blood pressure) Paracetamol (pain) Amlodipine (blood pressure) Salbutamol (asthma) Bendroflumethiazide (blood pressure) Lansoprazole (stomach acid)

The NHS does restrict what can be supplied on an NHS prescription, and I do agree that the NHS should not fund my malaria tablets (when I'm affording to jet off somewhere exotic) but I don't agree with Gluten Free bread / pizza / biscuits / muffins… all being allowed on an NHS prescription.

(£1.75 plus postage and wholesaler charges costs about £20 for a packet of GF bourbon biscuits!)

Confessions of a Chemist

GF bread (that you can buy nowadays in the supermarket) is no more expensive than a regular loaf and none of us are supposed to eat much bread.

I know this because my dad tried a touch-screen diet-and-lifestyle life-expectancy calculator in his GP surgery, and it wouldn't accept his answer (TEN slices) for how much bread he ate per day.

ERROR

Patients with GF requirements should have to pass a similar test before their prescription is issued by the surgery.

NO you cannot have biscuits AND muffins. Not only are they extortionate but they're not healthy. Buy some FRUIT like the rest of us.

ABUSE

Mrs Fury (who reminded me of a retired school headmistress with her hair in a bun, tweed skirt, and glasses) accused me of supplying her teenage daughter with the morning after pill. (Emergency Hormonal Contraception)

"The authority of God takes priority. As a Christian I am guided by the Scriptures which forbid physical harm of the innocent. Abortion is killing a person in an act of selfishness. Parents have a responsibility to help their children protect themselves from harmful behaviours such as promiscuity" she said, not thinking to thank me – thank me for educating her daughter on how to put a condom on, screening her for chlamydia…

Hell, it was me that encouraged her to tell her parents for god's sake woman.

"OK" I said, after her rant. "But I still can't talk to you about whether I did or did not supply the morning after pill to your daughter – for reasons of confidentiality." *How many days would it have taken your daughter to pluck up the courage to tell you?*

By then, the effectiveness would have dropped from 95% to about 50% after 72 hours.

So there's a good chance I've saved another unwanted teenage pregnancy.

After she'd gone, I made additional notes about the mother on the original consultation form (which must be held for 25 years) and I imagined an alternative outcome – had the daughter asked the mother to accompany her to the pharmacy in the first place. I imagined an unwanted orphan turning up at my counter in 25 years' time saying "I've been raised by a witch of a grandparent because my mother never wanted me. Why did you refuse the supply?"

In the same way a child throws a tantrum, I've come to expect abuse from drug addicts when they don't get what they want. Although a child of tantrum age probably wouldn't spit in your face or threaten you with a knife. *To be fair, as a caffeine addict I'd be pretty pissed off if someone stood between me and my morning cuppa.* But quite often perpetrators of abuse are not the usual suspects.

Mr Creepy was an old man who'd taken a shine to me. He fetched me his deceased wife's garter. "I thought you'd like it" he said. *Is this classed as sexual harassment?* Mr Impatient stood up out of his wheelchair and threatened to hit me with his walking stick because his prescription was still at the doctors. *Good job the counter stands between us.*

The fear of abuse can be dreadful. Imagine what it feels like locking up pharmacy premises, often in the dark, and walking to your car with the keys to the sweet shop! That's another reason why I prefer working inside a supermarket. Security would have escorted Mr Impatient from the building and banned him from shopping there again – had he dared hit me with his walking stick.

The pharmacist was ready to pour the methadone. She'd printed all the labels and stuck them on the bottles ready to dispense the benchful of daily methadone prescriptions. She went to open the controlled drug cabinet and couldn't find the goddamn key. She'd had it twenty minutes ago when she'd opened up at 7am but she couldn't find it anywhere. PANIC set in – such was the fear of not being in a position to supply methadone to these addicts. She had an hour before any of them would show up. *What to do for the best?*

That hour passed to no avail. CCTV footage showed her turning the computer on and opening the bottle drawer… but she didn't appear to have the key in her hand. There was only one thing for it – she'd have to break into the cabinet. Methadone patients started to arrive, and were kindly asked to come back in an hour 'when the delivery will have arrived.' Meanwhile the locksmith worked on opening the cabinet and changing the lock. *What a performance!*

Confessions of a Chemist

If she'd not been in a state of panic, at the thought of addicts kicking off, I've no doubt the pharmacist could have retraced her steps and found the key. I found the key the very next day – when I opened the bottle-drawer. "Aha. The missing key!"

Methadone patients don't often possess calendars to organise their chaotic lives. They need reminding when their two-week-prescription is close to running out. We try our best to remember to remind all of them, but if someone forgets I'll be faced with an angry addict. Not so if the Drugs Team is open because the methadone patient can simply pick up their next prescription, but come evening time it's me against the world.

With late-opening pharmacy come late-night dilemmas. Drunken methadone patients pose a particular dilemma. *To supply or not to supply?*

That is the question. A question that no-one can help a community pharmacist answer outside of normal working hours. The Drugs Team are closed. The patients GP surgery is closed. And before I push the panic button (with a two-fingered feel-good push like you're poking the offender in the eye) I have this to consider:

If I supply methadone to this already intoxicated patient (who's therefore more likely to overdose) and they expire, then I can be charged with manslaughter.

If I refuse the supply, on the grounds that they are intoxicated (with alcohol or other substance) they might use street-drugs instead of their methadone, and expire. *Could the family accuse me of indirectly causing the death of their loved one by refusing to supply?* Absolutely they could and I'd have to prove otherwise – prove that my actions were not negligent.

A doctor from The Drugs Team once reassured that I could never kill a patient by not supplying because withdrawals are unpleasant but not life-threatening. With that in mind, I decide I'll sleep easier if I refuse the supply.

Who would like to be the one who has to tell him/her that they can't have their methadone until they sober up?

Confessions of a Chemist

Flu Jabs

My colleague and I have administered approximately 500 flu-jabs between us this winter – thankfully without a single fainter or anaphylaxis.

At risk groups can have their flu-jab for free. (Inc. those over 65years, pregnant, serious medical condition, long-stay residential care, the main carer, frontline health/social care workers.) If you've been to the doctors for yours then you will have seen how quickly the nurses immunise their waiting-roomful of patients.

It crossed my mind (when we were doing so many that I was giving flu-jabs in my sleep) that it was so quick and easy *I could jab a patient in the consulting room before they'd had time to explain they hadn't actually come for a flu-jab.*

Scared of needles, I'm not sure how the company persuaded either of us to offer the service. If I tell you we practiced on oranges, it may not surprise you to know that I swore the first time I injected a real arm. Weirdly that wasn't the first time I've injected an orange. I tried injecting them with vodka to take to the V Festival, but I wouldn't try it at home because it just squirts back out of the holes.

My colleague progressed from an orange to her mum, and she cried before administering that first flu-jab. One of the Karens kindly volunteered to be my guinea pig, in return for a free flu-jab. So hesitant was my shaking hand that the needle touched her arm without puncturing the skin "F*ck!"

Too many men for my liking have come for their flu-jab wearing long shirts. "Can I have a fresh vaccine" asked one, like he was getting fish&chips.

"I don't want last season's" he said, unbuttoning his shirt.

Not wishing to see their naked torso, I was tempted to ask them to come back with suitable easy-arm-out clothing, but we were chasing our target of 500 and I thought *they might not come back.*

It was not unusual for couples to come in together, but I couldn't believe one man wanted his wife to hold his hand – and she did.

"Do I get a lollypop?" asked a grown man, after his flu-jab.

"Got any Disney plasters?" asked another.

To be honest I would have expected more stories to tell, after giving hundreds of flu-jabs, but then it is a very quick and relatively painless injection.

Confessions of a Chemist

Is that why the women take it in their stride?
Do women compare everything to childbirth?

"Must I make an appointment for a flu-jab?" asks one customer.

"No, we're pleased to be able to offer a walk-in service this year. Would you like one now?" I ask.

"No thanks. I've had one this year" he says, and walks off. *Eh?*

Shit the Bed

Never attempt to catch a falling knife

Behind every silly safety warning is a person suing for not being warned otherwise. Not everyone bothers to read instructions. Similarly not all patients read the patient information leaflet supplied with their medication.

Not reading the leaflet can put patients at a disadvantage. The well-known example being: **Remove the suppositories metal foil before inserting**. Not reading the label is also a mistake.

"But no-one told him not to swallow them!" Mrs Gulp shouted at Karen for not verbally telling her husband not to SWALLOW his suppositories. You might assume this advice is unnecessary. So why does the packaging on my thermometer read: **Once used rectally the thermometer should not be used orally**?

I'd like to think even if your eyesight is poor common sense might prevail on this one but evidently some directions are not clear enough. **Heat in the microwave for 3-5 minutes.** After 35 minutes the microwaveable wheat-bag was on fire!

Insert contraceptive cap at night, remove and wash every morning. She'd followed the doctor's directions, so why was she pregnant? Her husband works nights!

As a pharmacist, I endeavour to help patients get the best from their medication. This can be in the form of a Medicines Use Review (MUR) where I sit down with regular patients and discuss how they use of their medication.

MURs are optional Advanced Services whereas all pharmacies must offer Essential Services such as dispensing and promoting healthy lifestyles. An MUR may be offered to a patient who has received prescriptions from us for at least three consecutive months and over 2 million MURs were conducted in England 2011/12.

An MUR is a medication review focussing on a patient's understanding and use of their medication – with the aim of improving patient knowledge / adherence and reducing wastage. It is an opportunity for patients to ask questions.

Nowadays we need a signed patient consent form before an MUR. *Naturally I'll ask for your signature after the MUR or you'll never agree to talk to me.*

When as many as half of patients don't use their medication as directed by their doctor, MURs potentially save the NHS money – they also result in funny anecdotes.

MURs can identify potential side effects:

Taking senna laxative tablets in the morning rather than at night because "What if I shit the bed?" no-one had explained how the tablets work overnight.

Problems using their medication:

Using scissors every morning to cut capsules out of a blister pack because they are "Impossible to pop out" until I demonstrate how to simply peel the foil back.

Medication they no longer need:

"I order them every month because I don't want the doctor to know I don't take them or he'll think I'm a bad patient"

Whether or not they understand how to correctly use their medication:

"Can you show me how you use your inhaler?" I asked one patient, who was allergic to a new dog and become slightly asthmatic.

"I haven't got the dog with me" he replied. Unbelievably, he'd been spraying the dog!

Why they need to take their medication:

One gentleman had not started taking his new blood pressure tablets because he thought they were ten times stronger than his old ones – and the weak ones made him ill "But these 50mg must be stronger. My old tablets were only 5mg" (*Wrong!*) Consequently his blood pressure had gone sky-high.

Mr Repetitive once had one ten-minute MUR with myself, and never let us forget it. Every month he'd hand his prescription in, and tell us he'd "already had the Spanish Inquisition."

I think he thought it was funny but Karen got tired of listening to his broken record and pointed out the MUR had been for his benefit "You won't get that service everywhere you know" she told him. When he'd gone, I said "Look, this explains it Karen" pointing to his prescription including laxatives "He's full of crap."

It can be very difficult being patient-centric all day every day. We don't offer these additional services because we're all stood around doing nothing. Prescription volume continues to rise and at the same time we offer MUR's, morning-after-pills, Ventolin inhalers, flu-jabs, cholesterol checks, smoking cessation clinics... *Next thing you know (with the obesity epidemic) I'll be walking round the supermarket advising customers what to put in their trolley!*

We help Mrs Peg manage her weight. Karen weighs her every Monday and she's lost three stone in as many years. She would have lost more if she didn't go and celebrate a good weigh-in with a cream cake in the customer café. What we can't help her with is her sense of smell. "Got a peg?" Karen used to ask me – for her nose. *It's a mystery how someone can be that urine-scented and remain oblivious to it. Bless her.*

The human brain spends a lot of time on auto-pilot. Ever walked back to your car because you can't recall pressing the key-fob to lock it? To avoid daydreaming when busy/tired/stressed/all of the above, I talk out-loud (to engage the left side of my brain) as I'm checking prescriptions. "Right patient. Right dose. Right tablet. Right strength. Right label. Right quantity. Right bag..."

So should you hear me talking to myself, this does not indicate I've gone mad. Try it for yourself next time you leave the house. "Front door is locked"

Pressure turns into stress when you feel unable to cope. This usually happens when we are short-staffed and at times like that I don't know whether to laugh; cry; pull the shutters; or run away?

The fact you have frozen food in your trolley, and a taxi waiting, will not make your prescription appear any quicker. "What's taking so long? It's only a box of tablets!"

And if you're rude, there's every chance it'll take longer so don't be so quick to impatiently tap your fingers on the counter. This is not the Deli counter. If you rush me I might make a mistake then you'll really have something to shout about.

One of the shopful-of-customers wants to ask me something. "I can see you're very busy" she says. *Yes. I'm full-bladdered-busy* (meaning I daren't go for a toilet break, and return to find the benchful-of-prescriptions has multiplied in my absence) *but you're going to tell me your life story anyway aren't you?*

Mrs Under-Tall is a middle aged mum wanting something for her teenage daughter. Her chunky legs are red raw at the tops from rubbing together when she walks *I doubt she runs anywhere.* We have an anti-chafing gel but it's nearly £10 and as I explain it won't solve the problem. "Well I'm not buying something that won't work" says mum. And I kindly explain she'll have to buy it forevermore unless her daughter loses weight.

I offer them free diet and lifestyle advice but "I can't stop her from eating" says mum. "No but you choose what food to buy. Could you cut something out like crisps?" I suggest, looking at their trolley – full of all the wrong stuff. "What about the rest of us?" asks Mrs Under-Tall. "Small changes can make a big difference" I say, looking at her son tucking into a Mars bar as we speak.

"How about only having chips once a week?" I suggest.

"Once a week? I have chips twice a day. Once at school and once at home" admits the daughter.

I'm thinking to myself this is beyond my remit. But maybe, the doctor the school nurse and me, maybe we can have a cumulative effect and save this child from diabetes and heart disease?

Confessions of a Chemist

"Do you do any exercise? PE at school or anything?" I ask the daughter but I've visions of her sitting it out, while her classmates run around like children should.

"Her legs hurt too much" claims mum and I give up – for today at least.

Everyone likes to feel appreciated.

'Taking everything into account, was the service you received today very good/ fairly good / fairly poor / poor?' One thing's certain I don't judge our patient satisfaction on the annual survey. We give them to the same 100 customers every year – regular customers we know and love. *Well at least I don't fill them in myself.*

Most customers haven't got time. I never have time when the bank clerk asks me to fill out their questionnaire. Customers might agree to it if we've saved them time and/or money with a free cholesterol check or a free consultation for malaria tablets... The customers signed up to our 'prescription collection' service daren't refuse my emotional bribery "Would you like us to collect your prescription from the surgery again next month? Well, could you take a minute to fill in a questionnaire for me please?"

Patient satisfaction shows in the lack of complaints.

A customer announces that she has a complaint. Karen says "I'll get the pharmacist" and tells me a customer wants to complain. *My heart sinks.* "How can I help" I ask the lady at the counter. "I've had a chronic stomach complaint for the last ten years…" says the woman. *Oh great. I mean Oh no poor you.*

The profession is calling for decriminalisation of dispensing errors but in the meantime we live in fear of criminal prosecution.

That's the main reason we hardly use our mortar and pestle anymore. Older members of the public, who still remember chemists in white lab-coats, occasionally ask "Can the chemist mix me something up?" But pharmacists fear making a mistake and being liable. So to avoid risk, when it comes to lotions and potions with special formulations, pharmacists use specials manufacturers and the internationally recognised symbol of pharmacy – the mortar and pestle – sits on the shelf gathering dust.

Sometimes customers tell me I've made a mistake, but it turns out they're mistaken.

Take Mr & Mrs Trendy for example. Off to Goa they came to me for malaria prophylaxis.

We sat together in the consultation room, Mr Trendy in his *Lacoste* top and Mrs Trendy with her *Gucci* handbag, calculating how many malaria tablets they'd need…

One question to the female in the room always elicits the same raised eyebrow response from the male "Any chance you could be pregnant?" *Does 'No chance' mean you don't do it anymore?*

The Trendy's returned to the pharmacy five minutes after paying for their tablets. "I thought you said we needed 16 malaria tablets? This is a box of 12 tablets" said the young woman.

"Yes but if you look, I've put an extra four tablets inside" I replied confidently, while she opened the box. "Oh yes I'm so sorry" she said.

At which point the husband held up his bag, smiled and said to me "Look, I trusted you!"

One mistake I'll never forget, was an easy mistake to make because father and son (Mr Smith and Mr Smith Senior) share the same first name.

Labelled on the wrong Patient Medication Record in error, Mr Smith Senior was not happy when we delivered his *ErectEase* device to his son. *Oops.*

I learnt a lot that afternoon.

For a start, I'd never seen a vacuum pump for erectile dysfunction before. They have constrictor rings to maintain the erection. Rings come in sizes 1-5 a choice of firm/regular and colour options of pink beige or grey. Grey I mused, *is that for the Fifty Shades fan?*

Confessions of a Chemist

Health & Safety

The Lancet general medical journal recently reported that having a highly demanding job, but little control over it, could be a deadly combination of job strain increasing the risk of cardiovascular disease. *Who said hard work never killed anyone?*

Community pharmacists rarely have proper lunch breaks. We should not eat in the dispensary either (for obvious hygiene reasons.) *Shhh* Don't tell anyone but I squirrel away biscuits in secret stashes, bury chocolate deep in drawers and disguise supplies of sweets as bagged-up prescriptions.

In a twelve hour day, I'm lucky to have thirty minutes away from the dispensary.

If it wasn't for the humble kettle, I might feel hard done to. Working long shifts in premises with no central heating, I've had chilblains from standing all day on concrete floors and dry skin from fan-heaters. Cooped up in a pharmacy with no windows or natural light, I've suffered from seasonal affective disorder.

If the kettle goes, I go.

Banished from the dispensary on the grounds of Health&Safety (because walking with my take-away coffee from the customer cafe – dodging children, mobility scooters and trolleys – is less of a risk) the pharmacy kettle was banned for a second time when someone (in another branch) spilled coffee over the computer.

One nonsensical rule under the guise of H&S and employees won't take the rest of the rules seriously.

Like anyone who's ever worked in a pharmacy, I know the importance of using a kick-stool correctly. We use it all day every day as a means to access high shelves. If you're not familiar with this versatile piece of equipment, that you kick to move, it is a stool on castors – which collapse onto a rubber base ring when any weight is placed on the kick-stool providing a solid platform to stand on.

I've seen with my own eyes, the consequence of careless a dismount/pirouette – when one of the Karens had a kick-stool related accident. Basically she failed to dismount slowly and carefully, one foot at a time. You might think two foot is not very far to fall – especially for a four-foot-nothing Karen – but she turned before she stepped down, fell to the floor and broke her arm!

Overly precautious procedures may even result in rebellious employees. For example: Only work at height (which includes the two foot high kick-stool) when other methods have been exhausted i.e. relocation of stock on high shelves.

If you do not have to go up there, don't.

Now imagine three Karens facing each other, and holding hands like 'a ring of roses' around a kick-stool. Each Karen puts one foot on the same kick-stool and lifts off the ground like a human pyramid on a motorbike... I can't say that ever happened!

Accidents can't always be predicted or prevented (assuming the equipment is used as intended and not faulty) they just happen. I know I'm not alone in thinking some dispensary drawers are not fit for purpose – as in they were designed by a leftie (who's never tried to open a drawer one-handed with a basket of medicines in the other hand.)

The drawers are not faulty, we'd report faulty equipment, but that didn't prevent one of the drawers opening unexpectedly and knocking one of the Karens out cold!

So try as the do-gooders might, to do away with our kettle, it makes a comeback. They don't see the wonders a brew can do for team morale.

If it came to it, I think I could argue that the kettle is good for business because caffeinated happy colleagues are more productive. But I just sneak a travel kettle back in to the dispensary, and over time, management forget about the ban.

In my experience, management tend to lose interest in the pharmacy never mind the kettle.

Confessions of a Chemist

The Humble Kettle

Please forgive me, let me stay.
Pharmacists need me, I make their day.
They work so hard, for so little reward.
To say I'm unsafe really is absurd.
Everybody owns one, they know what to do.
Everyone loves a cuppa (except maybe you)
I'll stay in the corner, out of the way.
Providing hot drinks, all day every day.
Water and soft drinks can't compare,
to freshly ground coffee in a cafétiere.
Pre-pack sandwiches are a bore.
Without me the Cup-a-soup is no more.
If you want a happy workforce,
my advice you will heed.
Bring the kettle back,
at lightning speed!
REALISE THIS
Resistance is futile.
I know you're The Boss but
tea and coffee rule.

EPILOGUE

A cardiovascular poly-pill is being developed, to reduce the risk of cardiovascular disease by reducing blood pressure and lowering cholesterol.

One in four people over the age of forty are prescribed a statin (for high cholesterol) by their doctor, but the suggestion is that everyone over fifty would take this one-a-day poly-pill regardless of their cardiovascular risk. *Will the NHS pay for this £1/day CV poly-pill?* I'm not sure the general public will buy it. No-one buys the cholesterol-lowering statin (for primary prevention) over-the-counter and that is cheap at half the price. *That's a lie, I sold one packet once.*

Like any good but unreimbursed charity the National Health Service could become bankrupt. Naturally we all want to live longer and with advances in medicine we are living longer, but new drugs are expensive and elderly people take more medication (as things start to degenerate.)

I've visited my grandparents in nursing homes. I've heard the elderly ladies refer to each other as "Ladies in waiting" as they're kept alive / kept waiting longer.

Was serial killer Dr Harold Shipman motivated to reduce his workload or ease the burden for the NHS (?) All lives are precious, but when resources are stretched to breaking point should it be a priority to prolong all life?

What with advances in medicine, a growing population and a growing elderly population, prescription volume continues to rise. The future could bring more vending machines and robotic dispensaries to supply our time-precious society with all this medicine. That might free up community pharmacists (allowing more time for patients) but don't robots usually lead to unemployment?

Perhaps the limited access patients have at late-night pharmacies after the shop has closed (with tannoys to talk to the pharmacist and hatches to hand out the medicine) will become as accepted as ePharmacy. And patients will email photos of their ailments (in the absence of a consulting room) for the pharmacist to make a virtual diagnosis via smartphone. Then again, if the NHS is privatised, we could see the return of old-fashioned inexpensive remedies mixed by pharmacists in white lab-coats. And we'll be called 'chemists' again.

How about I leave you with my prediction for the future of supermarket pharmacy?

I predict the most commonly asked question in supermarket pharmacy will remain unchanged.

"Can I have a pound coin for the trolley?"

THE END

Don't tell anyone but they're not really **Tablet Gods**

Keep the Secret **#lovegods**

Traditionally a gift for those in love, these clay figures with their exaggerated sexual organs are 'Los novios del Mojón' the couple from Mojón in Lanzarote.

Similar to giving an engagement ring – a boy would give one of the male figurines to a girl as a token of love and commitment. If she accepted, she would give him a female figurine as a seal of approval for marriage and they would live happily ever after *with or without Viagra*. The End.

I hope you enjoyed reading

Confessions of a Chemist

Please click Like, rate / review

Share it on Facebook and Twitter

You might like to read my other book
Romantic Comedy
Window Shopping For Men:
Buy One Get One Free (BOGOF)

Many Thanks

Jemima McCandless

Tell me – was it a recipe for laughs?

@JemimaMcC #RxLAUGHS

References

National Treatment Agency for Substance Misuse
http://www.nta.nhs.uk/news-2012-annualstatistics.aspx

The Information Centre for health and social care
National Statistics
General Pharmaceutical Services in England 2002-2003 to
2011-2012 Published 22 Nov 2012
www.ic.nhs.uk
Prescriptions dispensed in the community: England
Statistics for 2001-2011
www.ic.nhs.uk

Management of Paracetamol Overdose
http://www.mhra.gov.uk/home/groups/pl-
p/documents/drugsafetymessage/con184709.pdf

Point of Dispensing Checks
http://www.nhsbsa.nhs.uk/CounterFraud/Documents/PO
D_Counter_Aide.pdf

3447559R00070

Printed in Great Britain
by Amazon.co.uk, Ltd.,
Marston Gate.